Curiosity Didn't Kill the Cat, it Made Her CEO

> *I have no special talents.*
> *I am only passionately curious.*
> *– Albert Einstein.*

This book offers a fresh take on leadership. I personally felt that the book was advice for an average Joe on the street who dreams of becoming a CEO, one day. It provides practical advice on how to realize it with one secret ingredient - Curiosity. A must read for college students and mid-career professionals.

Chaitanya Bailey
Founder, Indic Strategy Consulting

This easy to read guide is a must read for those seeking to advance their professional careers. This book takes the reader through a journey of discovery, laying out fundamental advice and uncovers the art of asking the right questions to help you succeed in the workplace.

Avril McHugh
Technology Executive, Financial Services

Both Sheli Bowman and cats count among my favourite things. Love the premise of this book, and Sheli's wisdom is really worth reading. Highly recommend this as a go-to business guide.

Liz Moscrop
CEO, GearUp TV

Curiousity Didn't Kill the Cat, it Made Her CEO

A light, fun read with concrete tips and advice on being a better leader. There are many cultures and workplaces that fail to embrace curiosity, it's about time we frame it as a positive skill through which we can grow and make teams stronger. Go Aurora Tigris!
Camilla Zanzanaini
CEO & Founder, Nature Makers Lab

I wish I had this book by my side during my startup days as well as when we all moved on, when we all had to handle and develop leadership in the corporate world. It's concise, to the point, it provides those handy reference tips everyone needs whilst being PowerPoint free. For any cool cat out there, its Purr-fect.
Mel Christie
Senior Director, SAP, mentor and leader

Love it. Fun, creative, empowering, thought-provoking. A brilliant and creative take on curiosity and the importance of curiosity for better solutions, innovation and to improve our relationships.
Monica Browning
Founder, Courage Through Coaching

Curiosity Didn't Kill the Cat, it Made Her CEO

Mastering the Power of Inquisitive Leadership

Sheli Bowman

Copyright @ Brand Catalyst Limited 2024

The right of Sheli Bowman to be identified as the author of this work has been asserted by her in accordance with the Copyright, Designs, and Patents Act 1988.

All rights reserved. No part of this publication may be reproduced, stored in a retrieval system, or transmitted in any form or by any means without the prior written permission of the author, nor be otherwise circulated in any form of binding or cover other than that in which it is published and without a similar condition being imposed on the subsequent purchaser.

ISBN: 9798332014864

Imprint: Independently published, Brand Catalyst Limited

Dedication

This book is dedicated to the CEOs of our family, the inspirational women who have always nurtured my curiosity. Joanie, my Mom, was a dynamic force of nature who loved intensely and with a full heart not only my sister Gina and me but just about every child she ever met. My Grandma Ruth always encouraged me to live a life that made me happy, even if that meant traveling and living on the other side of the planet most of my life. My life motto, "I want my flowers before I die," comes from her. My Grandma Eva was full of childlike curiosity and joy in her own very special way. Even though they are beyond this veil, I know they are with us.

Table of Contents

Introduction: Curiosity Killed the Job Description 2

1. The Art of Asking Anything (Without Getting Fired.. .8

2. Interrogation Techniques for the Modern Leader 14

3. The Perfect Balance: Mastering Open-Ended and Closed-Ended Questions 22

4. Questioning Your Way to Brilliance (or at Least Better Ideas) 30

5. The Fine Art of Curiosity-Driven Feedback 38

6. Embrace the Unknown: Lead with Questions When You Don't Have All the Answers 46

7. Staying Curious: How to Keep Questioning Even When You Think You're the Cat's Meow 54

8. Cultivating Your Team's Potential, Not Just Their Performance 62

Final Thoughts: Questioning Your Way to the Top 68

Curiousity Didn't Kill the Cat, it Made Her CEO

Appendix

Top Cat Tips..i

How To Make Friends & Be Purrsuasive viii

About the Author x

Coming Soon! xii

*Creativity is based on the
belief that there's no particular
virtue in doing things the way
they've always been done.
– Rudolph Flesch*

Curiousity Didn't Kill the Cat, it Made Her CEO

The Genesis of this Book

Curiosity has been the guiding compass behind most of what I do - from my childhood questioning nature to my current entrepreneurial pursuits. Though I'll admit, there were times when "just get it done" or "that's how we've always done it" stifled my curiosity.

However, I've come to clearly see the difference between letting curiosity gather dust versus truly embracing it. It's the distinction between merely existing and truly thriving.

When I started sharing about the power of curiosity and inquisitive leadership on social media, the overwhelming response told me there's a thirst for more on this topic. So that's why I'm here - to share everything I've discovered about harnessing your natural curiosity for personal and professional success.

This isn't your typical dry business book. Instead, it's a curiosity-driven journey filled with pragmatic insights, actionable steps, and the occasional giggle. Because curiosity is anything but dull - it's the spark of creativity, the fuel driving us forward, and the enchantment that transforms the mundane into the spectacular

Curiousity Didn't Kill the Cat, it Made Her CEO

Introduction

Curiosity Killed the Job Description

Riddle me this: What do great leaders and curious cats have in common?

More than you might think!

Being a great leader is more than just knowing all the answers. It also comes from knowing how to shine a light in dark corners. It's about juggling knowledge with a ravenous drive for learning.

But wait, isn't that a contradiction?

How do you be the manager who knows it all yet preserves the wide-eyed wonder of a kitten?

That's where agile thinking's strength resides. And no agility surpasses that of a cat!

Curiousity Didn't Kill the Cat, it Made Her CEO

Would you like to be seen as the sultan of strategy, the emperor of creativity, and the legendary leader of your team? How do I get there? By harnessing your inner cat and welcoming curiosity (of course, with a bit of killer instinct),.

Forget about barking instructions (leave that for the dogs). Rather, use your knowledge to probe smart questions that directly address the issues at hand. Use the messy but awesome force of inquiry to open fresh thoughts, possibilities, and opportunities.

The true leadership hack is not always having all the answers. Sometimes you need to work backwards to find the question that will lead you to the solution. You will need to be inquisitive enough to investigate several routes, even if you end up in unanticipated places.

So be the inquisitive cat that constantly lands on her feet. If you welcome the insights that curious leadership offers, you will see your company and team flourish. Learn how to ask the questions and still have all the answers, or start with the answer and then work out the question that got you there.

And if you're going to think like a cat, you're going to need a cat guide.

Meet Aurora P. Tigris, a curious cat padding her way through the corporate jungle. We'll see how she went from catching mice in a quirky little startup to questioning her way to the top. While her feline colleagues preferred catnaps to collaboration, Aurora couldn't stop asking questions and finding answers. Why were they using this strategy? How could they streamline operations? What was the

Curiosity Killed the Job Description

long-term vision?

Her incessant inquiries raised some hackles. "Quit nosing around and just catch mice," they grumbled. "Let the humans worry about the big picture." But Aurora sensed her probing questions were more than just philosophical kibble; they were the catnip that could stimulate the company to reach its potential.

And then something extraordinary happened. Aurora's questions began sparking change. The humans took notice of her insights. Her ideas propelled innovation and progress. In the blink of a cat eye, Aurora clawed her way up to the top, eventually claiming the coveted corner office as CEO.

Was it her sleek coat and confident purr that earned her the executive title? No, it was her unbridled, unabashed curiosity.

Aurora's tale may sound like a fanciful yarn (and cats do love yarn), but it's rooted in a powerful truth: Questioning is the secret weapon of extraordinary leaders. In an era of blink-and-miss-it change and head-spinning complexity, the most agile and adaptive leaders are the ones who actively nurture their curiosity. They relentlessly seek fresh perspectives, hunt down hidden assumptions, and dare to ask "Why?" and "What if?"

Make no mistake, embracing curiosity requires a lion's courage. It means admitting you don't have all the answers. It invites messiness and ambiguity. It can lead you down some rabbit holes. But it's a non-negotiable for cutting-edge leadership.

Why is questioning such a potent catalyst? For starters, it taps into the collective intelligence and experience of your team. Even the sharpest leader can't match the knowledge held by an entire organization. By drawing out people's ideas through artful inquiry, curious leaders can unearth breakthrough solutions.

Additionally, questioning is a stealth influence strategy. Thoughtful questions can shape people's thinking, steer their problem-solving, and inspire them to level up their game—all without having to strong-arm them. Asking instead of telling fosters trust and psychological safety, emboldening people to take smart risks.

But here's the catch:. Not all questions are created equal. Slapping a question mark on the end of a sentence doesn't automatically make you an inspirational leader. Curious leaders must master the art and science of framing powerful questions. They need to know what types of questions to ask and when. And they must have the guts to listen to the answers, even when they're unsettling.

In this rollicking romp of a book, we'll explore how to wield questioning as a leadership superpower. We'll dissect the psychology of why questions motivate and mobilize like nothing else. We'll unpack the anatomy of brilliant questions and how to craft them. And we'll steal a peek inside the playbooks of the world's most curious leaders to see how they use questions to summon the full genius of their organizations.

Along the way, we'll nerd out on some organizational

psychology, swap juicy boardroom war stories, and pick up some tips from our feline hero, Aurora. So sharpen your claws and get ready to embrace your inner question mark.

Because in an increasingly complex world, curiosity didn't kill the cat; instead, it crowned her CEO.

Are you ready to reject "business as usual" and welcome a more curious, creative, and rewarding way of life and leadership? Buckle up for a curiosity quest to make even the Cheshire Cat grin. Let the cat games begin!

*Life loves to be
taken by the lapel and told,
'I am with you, kid. Let's go.'
– Maya Angelou*

Curiousity Didn't Kill the Cat, it Made Her CEO

1

The Art of Asking Anything (Without Getting Fired)

"Cats desire certainty, which can seem odd since we can seem to be such capricious creatures. But think about it: some say the glass is half empty, some say it's half full.

Cats tend to make certain that it's now 100% on the floor.

I learned to find a way to achieve certainty without spilling the proverbial glass of milk."

Tigris, Aurora (2022), Five Habits of Highly Furry People

Ah, the delicate dance of wielding questions wisely as a leader. It's like juggling flaming torches while unicycling on a tightrope. One false move, and you could singe your eyebrows or plummet into the abyss of unemployment.

But fear not, my fellow felines of inquiry! In this chapter, we'll explore how to finesse your questioning to extract critical intelligence, inspire innovative ideas, and influence your team to greatness—all without leaving scorch marks on your employee file. It's time to learn the art of asking anything without getting fired.

First up, let's talk about the different flavors of questions in your leadership toolkit. Just like a master chef selects specific ingredients to concoct a mouthwatering dish, curious leaders must mix and match questioning strategies to cook up organizational magic.

Want to gather some sneaky reconnaissance on your team's stickiest challenges? Toss out some open-ended "what" and "how" questions to get them gabbing. Craving a heaping helping of creative solutions? Whip up some "what if" and "how might we" queries to get their innovation juices flowing. Need to take the team's temperature on progress and metrics? Serve up some pointed diagnostic questions to gauge their grasp of goals and gaps.

But here's the rub. Questioning is a potent elixir that must be administered artfully. Too many probing questions delivered with wide-eyed intensity, and you could come off like an interrogator shining a bare light bulb in your team's eyes. Too few, and you miss opportunities to mine their insights and spark eureka epiphanies. The key is to sprinkle questions throughout your conversations like a dash of catnip—enough to pique and energize but not overwhelm.

It's also about the WAY you ask. Adopt an authentic tone of curiosity, not accusation. Frame questions as collaborative explorations, not gotcha grillings. And when the answers start flowing, put on your best listening ears. Lean in, nod encouragingly, and let them unspool their thoughts fully before chiming in.

Skeptical that a few little questions can really supercharge your leadership? Let's geek out on some psychology to understand why questions are bona fide brain boosters.

When you lob a well-crafted question at someone, it's like tossing a mental hot potato. Their brain reflexively catches it and starts tossing around ideas to formulate a response. Neurons start firing, perspectives start shifting, and suddenly they're seeing the problem or possibility through a whole new lens. It's like intellectual improv, with your questions as the prompts that get their mental gears whirring.

What's more, by inviting your team into the question-storming process, you're signaling respect for their smarts and giving them a stake in shaping the path forward. That builds engagement and shared ownership way more than simply barking marching orders.

But lest we forget, not all questions serve equally

noble purposes. Some leaders wield "gotcha" questions like a fencing sword, trying to skewer unsuspecting employees with their own words. Others ask disingenuous questions where they've already decided the answer, using faux inquiry as a flimsy veil for command and control. Don't be that guy. Questioning should be a tool for empowerment and illumination, not manipulation and browbeating.

Ultimately, the art of asking anything is all about intentionality and finesse. Know why you're asking the question. Anticipate how it might land. Have the guts to genuinely listen to the answer. And always, always stay curious.

Take our clever kitty, Aurora. As she rose through the ranks to top dog—er, cat—at her company, questioning was her leadership catnip. But she didn't just fling random queries into the wind and hope something useful would blow back.

She'd slink up to colleagues and purr, "I've been scratching my head about why our sales are slumping. What's your take?" She'd pounce on project updates with an inquisitive chirp: "Catch me up on the latest customer feedback. What themes are you hearing?" In meetings, she'd knead the conversation with nudges like, "How might this idea look in action?" or "What risks should we sniff out before we pounce?"

By weaving questions artfully into the fabric of her leadership, Aurora didn't just get smarter; she got results. Her well-timed whys and what-ifs unearthed buried obstacles, inspired ingenious pivots, and galvanized her team to claw their way to the top.

So take a page from Aurora's (coloring) book. Start sprinkling some strategic questions into your own leadership repertoire. Play with different types and tones, always grounding your inquiries in genuine curiosity. The answers you elicit may surprise you, energize you, even dazzle you.

Will it feel a bit awkward and messy at first? Probably. Like anything worth mastering, questioning with confidence takes practice and finesse. But bit by bit, question by question, you'll sharpen your skills and summon your team's most scintillating thinking.

And if you ever feel your questioning mojo wavering, just remember our girl Aurora. If that spunky little kitty can question her way from Mouse Catcher to Head Honcho, you can certainly learn to ask anything (well, maybe not for a belly rub).

So go on, get out there and start asking. Be brave, be bold, and be relentlessly curious. Who knows? With some well-crafted questions, you might just lead your team to the most spectacular heights—and the biggest bowl of kitty treats—they've ever seen.

Remember, a wild cat once asked,

"Will the humans allow me to sit by their fire and feed if I go "purr purr" and allow them to stroke my chin?"

It's been over ten thousand years and humans are still scooping their poop, so we know how well that line of reasoning went.

Curiousity Didn't Kill the Cat, it Made Her CEO

2

Interrogation Techniques for the Modern Leader

"Why do cats always land on their feet? Some say it's evolution, others claim there is a top secret feline circus training camp, and a few believe it comes from a sprinkling of magic kitty dust.

But the truth is way simpler: it's curiosity.

Curious cats don't leap blindly. They pause, look, and ask, "What will happen if I jump this way or that?"

They ponder, they wonder, and when all options have been taken in, they trust their instincts.

And that, my friends, is the secret to always landing on your four paws and not your face."

Tigris, Aurora (2022), The Tao of Meow

Alright, intrepid leader, you've mastered the basics of asking questions without getting the boot. Bravo! But now it's time to level up your inquiry game and venture into the untamed wilderness of probing for the truth, the whole truth, and nothing but the truth. Welcome to the wild world of interrogation techniques for the modern leader!

Before you start sweating bullets and having visions of dimly lit rooms and good cop/bad cop routines, relax. We're not talking about extracting state secrets or eliciting confessions of corporate espionage (though that would make for a juicy chapter, wouldn't it?). No, no, we're talking about deploying advanced questioning strategies to get your team to open up, spill the tea, and give you the unvarnished scoop on what's really going on in the trenches.

Why is this so crucial? Because, as a leader, you're only as effective as the information you're working with. If your team is feeding you a steady diet of sanitized sound bites and rosiest-scenario spin, you're flying blind. You need the raw, unfiltered, and sometimes uncomfortable truth to make smart decisions and steer the ship.

But here's the tricky bit: getting people to cough up that truth can be harder than getting a cat to cough up a hairball (trust me, I've tried). People have all sorts of reasons for holding back: fear of looking bad, worry about rocking the boat, and the desire to tell the boss what they think she wants to hear. Your job is to create an environment where the truth can come out and play.

Interrogation Techniques for the Modern Leader

How, you ask? By channeling your inner feline and getting curious, not furious. The goal isn't to back people into a corner and make them sweat; it's to invite them into a safe space and make them want to spill the tea.

First and foremost, you need to build rapport and trust. People won't open up to a leader they think might pounce on them for saying the wrong thing. So dial up your empathy, put on your best "I'm all ears" face, and make it crystal clear that you genuinely want to hear their unfiltered perspective, warts and all.

Once you've set that stage, it's time to start deploying some tactical questioning moves. One of my favorites is the "Help me understand" opener. Instead of asking, "Why did you miss the deadline?" try, "Help me understand what obstacles cropped up that made hitting the deadline tough." See how that flips the script from finger-pointing to problem-solving?

Another ninja move is the "How might we..." question. Let's say you suspect there's some simmering tension between two teams that's throwing sand in the gears of progress. Instead of asking, "What's the beef between you two?" try, "How might we foster more collaboration and shared wins across our teams?" That little reframe invites them to trade gripes for solutions.

You can also try the classic "What's keeping you up at night?" question to surface lurking concerns or the "If you were in my shoes..." hypothetical to suss out what they really think should happen. The beauty of these questions is that they give people permission to speak candidly without fear of backlash.

Now, I know what you're thinking—what if, despite your best efforts, you're still getting the sanitized version of the truth? That's when it's time to pull out the big guns and go full-on Sherlock Holmes.

Pay attention to nonverbal cues. Does someone get fidgety when you ask about a certain topic? Do they avert their eyes or start speaking in generalities? Those are all clues that there's more to the story. Use follow-up questions to gently prod and see if you can get them to crack.

You can also try the "I've heard..." technique, where you reference a piece of intel you've picked up (even if it's just a hunch) and see how they react. "I've heard some rumblings that our new product launch is running into snags. What's your take?" If they get defensive or cagey, that's a sign you're onto something.

And if all else fails, there's always the trusty silence trick. Ask a probing question and then just sit there, letting the silence stretch out like a lazy cat in a sunbeam. You'd be amazed how often people rush to fill that awkward void with juicy tidbits they might otherwise have held back.

But here's the important disclaimer: with great questioning power comes great responsibility. These techniques are not to be used for petty gossip-mongering or witch hunts. The goal is always, always to surface truth in service of making things better—for your team, your organization, and your customers.

Interrogation Techniques for the Modern Leader

Lest you doubt the power of artful interrogation, let's take a peek at a few leaders who've elevated it to an art form.

Take Indra Nooyi, the former CEO of PepsiCo. She was known for her "Socratic leadership" style, peppering her team with thought-provoking questions to stimulate debate and drive creative problem-solving. Her favorite one? "What would you do if you were me?" Talk about a perspective-shifting zinger!

Or consider Ray Dalio, the legendary founder of Bridgewater Associates. He's made "radical transparency" the cornerstone of his leadership philosophy, using piercing questions to surface problems and get to the heart of the matter. In meetings, he'll often go around the room and ask each person, "What do you think is the biggest weakness in my argument?" or "What am I missing here?" By modeling that relentless pursuit of truth, he's built a culture where people feel safe (and even obligated) to speak their minds.

And let's not forget our very own Aurora, the curious cat who clawed her way to the corner office. Her signature move was the "whisker twitch"— every time she sensed something was off, she'd cock her head to the side, twitch her whiskers, and ask a disarmingly innocent question that would invariably uncover the root of the issue. "I'm confused—why are we seeing such high customer churn this quarter?" twitch twitch "Help me understand why we're behind schedule on the XYZ initiative." twitch twitch. Her team quickly learned that when the whiskers started twitching, it was time to get real.

So there you have it, folks—the art of asking anything, part two. Interrogation techniques for the modern leader. Your secret weapon for cutting through the fluff and getting to the good stuff.

Remember, the goal isn't to be a hardass or a truth tyrant. It's to create a culture of candor where people feel safe speaking openly and honestly in service of doing great work together.

So go forth and ask boldly, my fellow felines. Channel your inner Aurora and let your curiosity be your guide. Who knows what juicy insights and aha moments await? Just try not to make too many suspects cry in the process. (Kidding!)

And even crying isn't all bad; how do you think Kleenex got invented?

Curiosity is unruly. It doesn't like rules, or, at least, it assumes that all rules are provisional, subject to the laceration of a smart question nobody has yet thought to ask. It disdains the approved pathways, preferring diversions, unplanned excursions, impulsive left turns. In short, curiosity is deviant.

- Ian Leslie

Curiousity Didn't Kill the Cat, it Made Her CEO

3

The Purrfect Balance: Mastering Open-Ended and Closed-Ended Questions

"Dogs respond well to closed-ended quetions. They seem to be happy with everything, e.g.:
"Wanna go for a walk?" ...YES!
"Who's a good boy?"...ME!
Cats deal well with open questions,
"Where did you find that giant dead bird?"
"What would be better than laser pointers?"
"Why do you keep biting me when I think we're actually friends?"
"How are you feeling about the new food?"
A tail flip and retreat to their favorite box mean these questions are not being entertained, while the Cheshire cat grin offers the answer.
Curiosity doesn't kill cats; it has their backs."

Tigris, Aurora (2023), Of Mice and Meal Times

Alright, my inquisitive friends, it's time to talk about the yin and yang of questioning—the delicate dance between open-ended and closed-ended queries. It's like the leadership equivalent of knowing when to use a laser pointer to focus your team's attention and when to bust out the catnip to get them romping and exploring.

Confused? Intrigued? Slightly hungry? Perfect. Let's dive in.

First, let's define our terms. Open-ended questions are the ones that invite expansive responses and creative thinking. They're the "tell me more" and "what do you think?" queries that get people riffing and riffling through possibilities. Closed-ended questions, on the other hand, are the ones that elicit a simple yes/no, either/or, or short factual response. They're the "did we hit our targets?" and "when will the project be done?" questions that nail down specifics.

Now, I know what you're thinking—isn't one type inherently better than the other? Aren't open-ended questions the cool cats of the questioning world, while closed-ended ones are the stodgy, fun-squashing hairballs?

Au contraire, my feline friend! Both types of questions have their place in the savvy leader's toolkit. The key is knowing when and how to use them for maximum impact.

Let's start with open-ended questions. These are your go-tos when you want to:

1. Encourage creative problem-solving: "How might we tackle this challenge in a way we

haven't tried before?"
2. Surface underlying issues or concerns: "What's the biggest obstacle you're facing in your work right now?"
3. Get a pulse on team morale: "How are you feeling about our progress so far?"
4. Invite diverse perspectives: "I'd love to hear everyone's thoughts on this—what are we missing?"

Open-ended questions are like catnip for the brain; they stimulate divergent thinking, encourage people to make unexpected connections, and can lead to breakthrough "aha!" moments. They signal that you value your team's ideas and insights, not just their ability to execute on yours.

But here's the thing: as powerful as open-ended questions are, they can also be a bit, well, unwieldy. Toss one out to a group and you might get a free-wheeling brainstorm that spans everything from "let's totally reimagine our business model" to "what if we replaced all our office chairs with yoga balls?" (Pro tip: don't do that last one. I did that with half the chairs in a start-up, and NO ONE used the yoga balls except for me. However, installing a big couch was a total winner with the yoga ball haters who couldn't find a chair! Just FYI)

That's where closed-ended questions come in. They're your trusty laser pointer, helping you focus the conversation and get concrete information. Use them when you need to.

1. Get a status update: "Are we on track to meet our Q3 goals?"

2. Confirm understanding: "Does everyone grasp the new process changes we just discussed?"
3. Make a quick decision: "Should we move forward with Plan A or Plan B?"
4. Gauge consensus: "Does everyone agree that this is our top priority?"

Closed-ended questions are like guardrails; they keep the discussion from veering too far off course and ensure you're getting the specific information you need to keep things on track.

But wield them too heavily and you risk shutting down discussion and making your team feel like they're being interrogated rather than engaged.

The secret sauce is in the mix: knowing when to use open-ended questions to invite exploration and when to use closed-ended ones to drive clarity and alignment.

One approach is to start broad and then narrow things down. Kick off a topic with an open-ended question to get the creative juices flowing, then use closed-ended follow-ups to zero in on key points. "What opportunities do you see for us to improve customer satisfaction?" might yield a smorgasbord of suggestions, which you can then drill down on with "Would implementing a new CRM system address the issues you raised?"

Another technique is to toggle between the two types based on the energy and focus of the group. If a conversation is starting to feel circuitous or unfocused, throw in a closed-ended question to bring it back to center. If things are feeling a bit stale or stuck, lob an open-ended query to inject some fresh thinking.

And don't forget the power of the follow-up probe. Regardless of whether you start with an open or closed question, be ready to dig deeper with a "say more about that" or "what makes you say that?" This is where you can really unearth hidden gems and get to the heart of the matter.

Now, I know this all sounds great in theory, but what does it look like in practice? Let's take a peek behind the scenes of some master questionnaires in action.

Remember our old friend Aurora, the curiosity queen turned top-cat CEO? One of her signature moves was "pounce and play"—she'd p pounce on a meaty topic with an open-ended question to get the conversational ball rolling, then bat it around with some playful follow-ups to keep things lively and uncover new angles.

In one legendary meeting, she started with "What's the boldest thing we could do this year to leave our competition in the dust?" which got her team excitedly riffing on everything from launching a new product line to sponsoring a cat fashion show (hey, don't knock it till you've tried it). But then she reined it in with "Which of these ideas would have the biggest impact on our bottom line?" which helped them prioritize their wild brainstorm into a concrete action plan. Pounce and play, folks. Pounce and play.

Or take Elon Musk, the enigmatic mastermind behind Tesla and SpaceX. He's known for his relentless questioning style, mixing open-ended whoppers with laser-focused follow-ups. In a now-infamous email to his employees, he once wrote, "I want to know what's actually going on in the factory. No sugar coating, no hiding behind complexity—just the unvarnished truth. What are the top 5 problems we need to solve to get production on track?" Talk about cutting through the fluff and getting to the heart of the matter.

And let's not forget Brené Brown, the acclaimed researcher and storyteller who's made a career out of asking courageous questions. Her secret weapon is the "tell me about a time when" question, which invites people to share vivid, vulnerable stories that illuminate universal truths. "Tell me about a time when you felt most alive at work" or "Tell me about a time when you had to have a tough conversation with a colleague"—these o open-ended doozies crack people open and forge deep, authentic connections.

So there you have it, folks—the art of asking anything, part three. Mastering the perfect balance of open-ended and closed-ended questions. It's not about picking one or the other, but knowing how to dance between the two in service of your goals.

Use open-ended questions to spark creativity, uncover insights, and build rapport. Use closed-ended ones to drive clarity, alignment, and action. And mix and match them like a maestro to keep your conversations fresh, focused, and fruitful.

And remember, asking brilliant questions isn't just about what you say, but how you listen. Be fully present, curious, and open to whatever emerges. The magic happens in the space between the question and the answer.

So go forth and query, my intrepid leaders. Channel your inner Aurora, Elon, or Brené, and let your questions be your superpower.

Who knows what astonishing answers await? Just try not to get too dizzy from all the intellectual acrobatics.

But as we cats show, acrobatics get easy with practice, just so long as you always land on your paws.

Curiousity Didn't Kill the Cat, it Made Her CEO

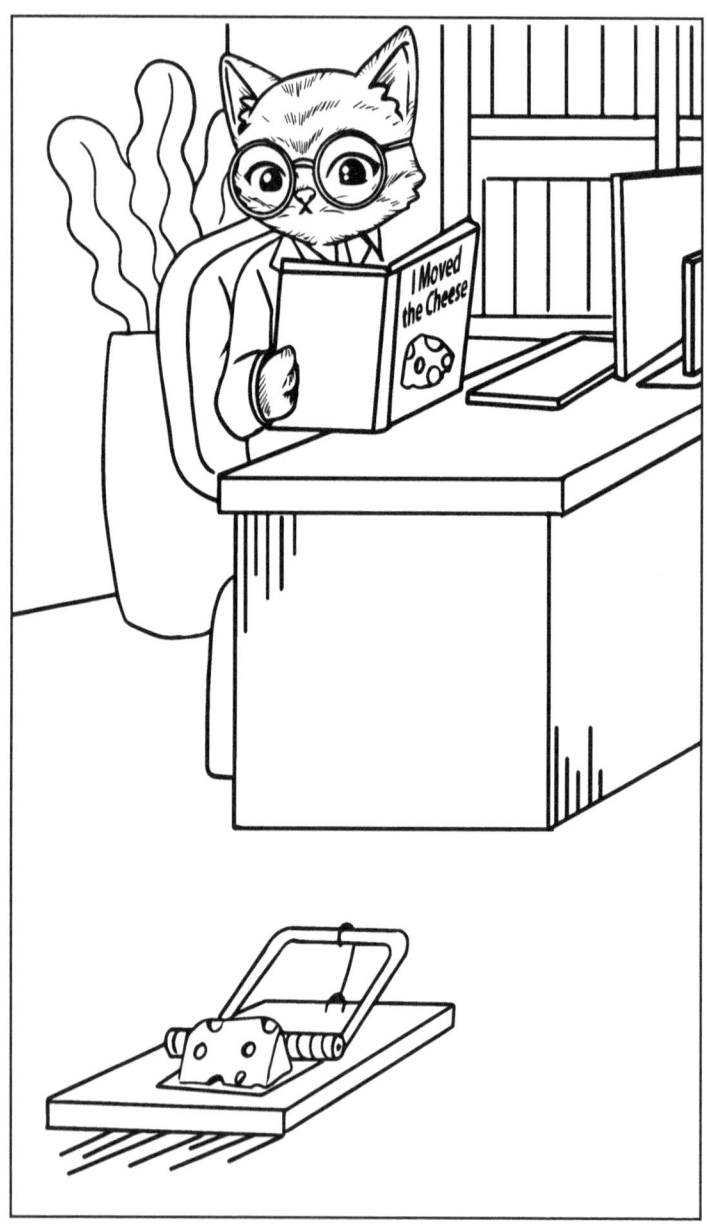

4

Questioning Your Way to Brilliance (or at Least Better Ideas)

"Are you ready for the biggest secret about cats? They don't actually have nine lives. Let me explain...

Mice may say, "Wow, someone left that nice piece of cheese under that spring-loaded steel bar, which means I get a free meal.".

Cats just look at the trap, sit back, and wait for a free meal to come to them.

Like a deliveroo cat treat.

Dogs chase balls and return them repeatedly, never once questioning the purpose of this action.

Cats trust nothing, question everything and because of that, it just seems like they get an extra eight lives."

Tigris, Aurora (1999), I Moved the Cheese

We're about to embark on a journey into the heart of creative questioning. That's right, we're talking about using the power of inquiry to unleash your team's most brilliant, audacious, game-changing ideas, or at the very least, some noticeably less terrible ones.

Now, I know what you're thinking. "But wait, isn't brainstorming just about throwing a bunch of half-baked notions at the wall and seeing what sticks?" Oh, you sweet summer child! If that's your approach, no wonder your "innovative" ideas are about as impressive as a cat's ability to resist a laser pointer (spoiler alert: not very).

No, no, my friend. True ideation magic happens when you wield questions like a wizard's wand, conjuring up sparks of inspiration and guiding your team through the creative labyrinth with finesse and flair.

But how, you ask? How do we question our way to brilliance without getting lost in a sea of absurdity or drowning in a pool of our own mental sweat? Fear not, for I have some tricks up my sleeve (and no, they don't involve actual magic wands, though I wouldn't say no to an enchanted laser pointer).

First and foremost, let's talk about the power of the "what if" question. This little two-word wonder is like catnip for your brain, enticing it to ponder possibilities that might otherwise seem too far-fetched or fantastical.

- "What if we could make our product invisible?"
- "What if we held our next team meeting on a

hot air balloon?"
- "What if we taught our customers to do handstands while using our software?"

Okay, maybe that last one is a bit much, but you get the idea. "What if" questions give your team permission to think beyond the realm of the practical and venture into the land of the imaginative. And who knows? Sometimes the most outlandish ideas can spark the most ingenious solutions.

Another favorite technique of mine is the "how might we" question. This one is like a trusty sidekick, helping you reframe challenges as opportunities and inviting your team to put on their problem-solving capes.

Instead of "we need to cut costs," try "how might we streamline our processes to be more efficient?" Instead of "our competition is eating our lunch," go with "how might we differentiate ourselves in a crowded market?" And instead of "nobody's buying our cat-sized top hats," aim for "how might we make our feline fashion more appealing to the discerning kitty buyer?"

See how those little linguistic tweaks can shift the energy from daunting to daring? "How might we?" questions are like a secret handshake that signals to your team's brains, "It's go time, gang. Let's figure this out together."

But here's the real secret sauce, the pièce de résistance, the catnip-coated cherry on top: the follow-up question. This is where you can really rev up the creativity engine and steer your team's ideas in bold new directions.

When someone tosses out a suggestion, don't just nod and move on. Probe deeper with questions like:
- "What's the most exciting thing about that idea?"
- "How could we make that even more impactful?"
- "What's the biggest obstacle we'd need to overcome to make that happen?"
- "What's the most unexpected way we could implement that?"

These follow-ups are like little nudges that encourage your team to stretch their thinking, consider new angles, and build on each other's brilliance. They create a sense of momentum and possibility, like a kitten chasing a string that keeps darting just out of reach (but in a good way, I promise).

Now, I know what you might be thinking. "But what if my team's ideas are terrible? What if they suggest we rebrand as a company that sells artisanal cat hair sweaters or start a line of tuna-flavored energy drinks?"

First of all, don't knock the tuna drinks until you've tried them. But more importantly, remember that the goal of creative questioning isn't to strike gold with every single idea. It's to create a space where people feel safe to explore, experiment, and even fail fantastically.

Some of the most game-changing innovations in history started as seemingly silly or far-fetched notions. The Post-It Note? It was invented by accident when a scientist was trying to create a super-strong adhesive. The Slinky? It was dreamed up by a naval engineer who was trying to create a device to keep ship instruments stable. And let's not even get started on the pet rock.

The point is, brilliance often masquerades as absurdity at first glance. Your job as a leader is to create an environment where those zany, half-formed, so-crazy-they-just-might-work ideas can come out to play without fear of judgment or ridicule.

So how do you do that? By modeling and creatively questioning yourself, of course! When you're brainstorming with your team, don't be afraid to toss out some wacky "what ifs" and "how might we's" of your own. Show them that it's not only okay to think outside the litter box; it's actively encouraged.

And when someone does offer up an idea that seems a bit, shall we say, unconventional, resist the urge to shoot it down or dismiss it out of hand. Instead, try a little "yes, and" magic. Build on their suggestion with an enthusiastic follow-up question or a playful twist that takes it in an even more intriguing direction.

Remember, the goal isn't to have all the answers, but to ask the kinds of questions that spark new ways of thinking and seeing. As the brilliant questionologist (that's a thing, right?) Warren Berger once said, "A beautiful question is an ambitious yet actionable question that can begin to shift the way we perceive or think about something—and that might serve as a catalyst to bring about change."

So go forth and question boldly, my curious compatriots. Channel your inner inquisitive kitten and let your "what ifs" and "how might we's" be your guide. And if anyone gives you flak for your unconventional ideas, just tell them you're on a quest for brilliance—or at least better ideas than the ones they've been coming up with. (Zing!)

Who knows what astonishing innovations await? Just try not to get too carried away with the tuna drink thing. Trust me on that one.

But be persistent; as the old cat proverb goes, "you have to poop in a lot of shoes before somebody invents a litter box."

You can't just give someone a creativity injection. You have to create an environment for curiosity and a way to encourage people and get the best out of them.
– Sir Ken Robinson

Curiousity Didn't Kill the Cat, it Made Her CEO

5

The Fine Art of Curiosity-Driven Feedback

"They say "curiosity killed the cat, but satisfaction brought her back", and it turns out that is true. This is going to be trickier in real life than you might think. If getting killed was an exam result, it would be one you rarely got to retake.
So how do you learn from experience without getting a terminal grade?"

Tigris, Aurora (2017), The Kibble Bowl Is Always Half Empty

Ah, feedback. The mere mention of the word can send even the bravest of souls scurrying for cover, like a cat caught in the act of shredding the living room curtains. But fear not, my intrepid leaders, for I come bearing glad tidings and a revolutionary approach to this oft-dreaded task: curiosity-driven feedback.

Now, I know what you're thinking. "Curiosity-driven feedback? Is that just a fancy way of saying, 'I'm curious to know how you managed to botch that project so spectacularly'?" But hold your judgmental horses, my skeptical friend. This isn't about wielding curiosity like a weapon to eviscerate egos and leave your team quivering in a puddle of their own inadequacy. No, no. This is about harnessing the power of genuine inquisitiveness to unlock growth, learning, and—dare I say it—even a little bit of fun.

You see, the problem with traditional feedback is that it often comes from a place of assumption and prescription. We think we know what went wrong and how to fix it, so we dispense our sage wisdom like a cat doling out hairballs (sorry, I couldn't resist). But here's the thing: our assumptions are often incomplete at best and flat-out wrong at worst. And when we prescribe solutions without fully understanding the context and perspective of the person we're talking to, we risk missing the mark and eroding trust in the process.

Enter curiosity-driven feedback. Instead of assuming and prescribing, this approach is all about exploring and discovering. It's about setting aside our preconceived notions and engaging in a genuine dialogue to uncover insights, lessons, and opportunities for growth—together.

So what does this look like in practice? Let's break it down, shall we?

Step 1: Check your assumptions at the door.

Before you even open your mouth to give feedback, take a moment to examine your own biases and beliefs. What assumptions are you making about the situation, the person, or the outcome? What "story" have you concocted in your head about what happened and why? Now, take a deep breath and let it all go. Like a cat shedding its winter coat (I promise, that's the last feline analogy for at least a paragraph), release your grip on those assumptions and open yourself up to the possibility that there might be more to the story than meets the eye.

Step 2: Lead with curiosity.

Instead of launching into a laundry list of what went wrong and what needs to change, start with an open-ended question that invites exploration and reflection. Something like,

- "I'm curious to hear your perspective on how things went with the XYZ project. What stood out to you as the biggest challenges and successes?"
- "Looking back on the presentation, what insights did you gain about your own strengths and areas for growth?"
- "I noticed that the team seemed to struggle with meeting deadlines this quarter. I'm wondering what you think might be

contributing to that pattern?"

See how those questions create space for dialogue and discovery? They signal that you're not here to lecture or condemn, but to learn and understand.

Step 3: Listen like a detective.

Once you've opened the door to curiosity, your job is to listen like your life depends on it. And I don't just mean nodding along while mentally planning your next brilliant insight. This means listening with your whole being—your ears, eyes, heart, and gut.

Pay attention not just to the words being said but also to the emotions, body language, and energy behind them. Listen for the unspoken fears, hopes, and dreams that might be driving behavior and shaping perspective. And resist the urge to jump in with your own thoughts and opinions. This is about creating space for the other person to process and explore, not about showcasing your own brilliance (though I'm sure it's dazzling).

Step 4: Ask follow-up questions.

As you listen, no doubt new questions and curiosities will arise. Don't be afraid to voice them! Follow-up questions are the secret sauce of curiosity-driven feedback, allowing you to dig deeper, challenge assumptions (both theirs and your own), and uncover new insights and possibilities. Some of my favorite follow-ups include:

- "I'd love to hear more about that. What do you think was driving that dynamic?"
- "That's interesting. How do you think that

impacted the outcome?"
- "I'm curious; what might have happened if you had approached it differently?"
- "What's one lesson you're taking away from this experience?"
-

Remember, the goal isn't to interrogate or put the other person on the spot, but to engage in a genuine exploration together. Think of it like a treasure hunt, where the treasure is a shared understanding and a path forward.

Step 5: Reflect and brainstorm together.

As you start to uncover insights and patterns through your curious questioning, the next step is to reflect on what you're learning and brainstorm ways to apply those lessons going forward. This is where the real magic happens—where feedback transforms from a one-way critique to a two-way dialogue about growth and possibility. Some questions to guide this phase might be:

- "Based on what we've discussed, what do you see as the key takeaways or lessons learned?"
- "How might you apply those insights to similar situations in the future?"
- "What support or resources do you need to put those ideas into action?"
- "How can I help you continue to build on your strengths and navigate challenges?"

Again, the key here is collaboration and co-creation.

You're not dictating a plan or prescribing a fix, but working together to chart a course forward based on a shared understanding of what's working, what's not, and what's possible.

And here's the real kicker: when you approach feedback with genuine curiosity and openness, it doesn't just lead to better outcomes and stronger relationships. It also makes the whole process a heck of a lot more enjoyable for everyone involved. Instead of feeling like a dreaded chore or an adversarial showdown, it becomes an opportunity for connection, learning, and growth. Who knows, you might even start to look forward to those feedback conversations! (Okay, that might be a stretch. But a cat can dream.)

Now, I know what you might be thinking. "This all sounds great in theory, but what about when the feedback is really tough? What if someone truly dropped the ball or needs a major course correction?"

Fair question, my astute reader. And the answer is that curiosity is still your friend. Even in the most challenging feedback scenarios, approaching the conversation with an open mind and a genuine desire to understand can make all the difference.

In fact, I'd argue that it's especially important in those high-stakes moments to resist the urge to assume, judge, or prescribe. That's when defensiveness and resistance are most likely to rear their ugly heads, and when a curious, collaborative approach can help keep things on track.

Of course, that doesn't mean you shy away from

The Fine Art of Curiousity-Driven Feedback

hard truths or fail to hold people accountable. But it does mean you seek to understand before seeking to be understood. You ask questions to get to the root of the issue, not to prove a point or assign blame. And you engage the other person in finding a solution, rather than dictating one from on high.

Here's the bottom line: curiosity-driven feedback is a game-changer. It's a way to transform a traditionally fraught and fear-inducing process into an opportunity for connection, learning, and growth. And all it takes is a willingness to set aside your assumptions, open your mind, and engage in a spirit of genuine inquisitiveness.

So go forth and be curious, my feedback-savvy friends. Channel your inner Sherlock Holmes and let your questions be your guide. Who knows? You might even start to look forward to those dreaded performance reviews!

Curiousity Didn't Kill the Cat, it Made Her CEO

6

Embrace the Unknown, Lead with Questions When You Don't Have All the Answers

"What do you say when you don't have the answer to an urgent question? Good question. No seriously, that's the answer "a good question." There's no such thing as a mouse you can't catch or a good question that can't be turned into a better answer."

Tigris, Aurora (2022), The 9 Habits Of Highly Furry People

Alright, my intrepid explorers, it's time to venture into uncharted territory of leadership—the land where questions are your compass and the unknown is your playground. That's right, we're talking about leading with questions when you don't have all the answers. And let's be real: when do you ever have all the answers? (If you do, please send me your secrets, because I've been winging it for years.)

We're halfway through the book, so I'm hoping you're not thinking: "But wait, isn't leadership about having all the answers? Isn't it about being the wise sage on the mountaintop, dispensing knowledge and certainty to the masses?" Because if that's your idea of leadership, you're not a leader; you're a fortune cookie.

Real leadership is about embracing the unknown, leaning into the discomfort of uncertainty, and having the courage to say those three little words that can strike fear into the heart of any self-respecting adult: "I don't know."

But here's the thing: not knowing is not a weakness. In fact, it can be your greatest strength if you know how to wield it like a lightsaber of curiosity and humility. And that's where leading with questions comes in.

You see, when you're faced with a challenge or a situation where you don't have all the answers (which, let's be real, is most of the time), you have a choice. You can either try to fake it till you make it, puffing out your chest and pretending you've got it all figured out (spoiler alert: no one's buying it). Or you can lean into the uncertainty and use it as an opportunity to learn, grow, and engage your team in a collaborative quest for solutions.

And that quest begins with questions. Not just any questions, but genuine, open-ended, curiosity-fueled questions that invite exploration, creativity, and critical thinking. Questions like:

- "What do we know about this situation so far, and what do we still need to learn?"
- "What assumptions might we be making, and how can we test them?"
- "What perspectives or expertise are we missing, and how can we bring them into the conversation?"
- "What are some potential approaches we could take, and what are the pros and cons of each?"

See how those questions create space for dialogue, discovery, and diverse viewpoints? They signal that you're not looking for quick fixes or easy answers, but for a deeper understanding of the problem and a collaborative exploration of possible solutions.

And here's the real magic: when you lead with questions, you're not just tapping into the collective wisdom of your team. You're also modeling a growth mindset and a willingness to learn that can be downright infectious (in a good way, not like that time Bob from accounting brought the flu to work and took out half the department).

Think about it: when your team sees you embracing the unknown and seeking out new perspectives and insights, they're more likely to do the same. They're more likely to take risks, think outside the box, and bring their full selves to the table. And that, my friends, is how you create a culture of curiosity, innovation, and continuous learning.

But wait, you might be thinking. "What if I ask a question and no one has the answer? Won't I look like a clueless leader who doesn't know what they're doing?"

First of all, let's get one thing straight: if you're a leader, you ARE a clueless leader who doesn't know what they're doing half the time. Welcome to the club; we all have jackets (they're invisible, but we know we're wearing them). Here's the important part, so grab your highlighter: not having the answer is not the same as not knowing what you're doing.

In fact, being able to say, "I don't know, but let's find out together" is a sign of true leadership strength. It shows that you're humble enough to admit when you're uncertain, confident enough to embrace the unknown, and courageous enough to lead your team into uncharted territory.

And here's the thing: your team doesn't expect you to have all the answers. They expect you to have the right questions. They expect you to create a space where it's safe to not know, to experiment, to fail, and to learn. They expect you to lead with curiosity, not with certainty.

So how do you do that? How do you cultivate a questioning mindset and create a culture of curiosity? Here are a few tips:

1. **Practice intellectual humility**

Recognize that you don't have all the answers, and

be willing to admit it. Embrace the idea that you have something to learn from every person and every situation, and approach challenges with a beginner's mind.

2. Ask more questions than you answer

Make a habit of leading with questions, even when you think you know the answer. Encourage your team to do the same, and create space for diverse perspectives and ideas to emerge.

3. Celebrate "I don't know."

When someone on your team says, "I don't know," don't see it as a failure or a weakness. See it as an opportunity to learn and grow together. Celebrate the courage it takes to admit uncertainty, and use it as a springboard for exploration and discovery.

4. Model curiosity

Be the kind of leader who's always asking "why?" and "what if?" and "how might we?" Show your team that it's not only okay to be curious, but that it's essential to success in a rapidly changing world.

5. Embrace the messiness

Leading with questions means embracing the messiness and discomfort of not having all the answers. It means being willing to try new things, to fail fast and learn from your mistakes, and to pivot when necessary. It's not always pretty, but it's always an adventure.

And that, my friends, is the heart of leading with questions—it's an adventure. It's a journey into the unknown, with curiosity as your compass and your team as your fellow explorers. It's a chance to discover new possibilities, to challenge old assumptions, and to create something extraordinary together.

So embrace the unknown. Lead with questions. And trust that the answers will reveal themselves along the way (or that Cindy from data analysis will find them in a random spreadsheet at 2am, because she's a data wizard and we don't deserve her).

But just remember, they put a dog in space first, because I suspect cats had a few more questions about the job description.

*Success in anything is just
a byproduct of learning, and
learning is a byproduct of curiosity.
Ultimately, if you are curious about
something, you will be successful
at it, and the more curious
you are about it, the more
successful you will be at it.*

- *Naval Ravikant*

Curiousity Didn't Kill the Cat, it Made Her CEO

7

Staying Curious: How to Keep Questioning Even When You Think You're the Cat's Meow

"Who's the top feline in the world? Lions right? King of the jungle? Well, where did you last see a lion? In a zoo, looking embarrassed, whilst a bunch of gawking tourists took photos of him. You don't see many curious cats anywhere they don't want to be, because they will never stop questioning...everything!"

Tigris, Aurora (2024), Be The Cat That Got The Creamery

Well now, look who's feeling like the big cheese, the top cat, the crème de la crème of the curiosity world. You've mastered the art of questioning, you've led your team to new heights of innovation and discovery, and you're starting to think you might just have this whole leadership thing figured out.

But wait, what's that sound? Is it the distant echo of complacency, the siren song of self-satisfaction? Or is it just your ego purring like a contented cat who's had one too many treats?

Don't get me wrong, my confident compadre. It's great to feel like you're on top of your game, like you've cracked the code and unlocked the secrets of the universe (or at least of your industry). But here's the thing about curiosity: it's not a destination; it's a journey. And the moment you think you've arrived—the moment you start resting on your laurels and admiring your own reflection—that's when you start to lose your edge.

You see, staying curious isn't about knowing all the answers. It's about always seeking new questions. It's about maintaining that sense of wonder and excitement that comes from discovering something new, even when you're at the top of your game. It's about resisting the temptation to get too comfortable, too complacent, or too darn pleased with yourself.

But how, you ask? How do you keep questioning when you feel like you've got it all figured out? How do you stay hungry when you're already the cat's meow? Fear not, my friend. I've got some strategies up my sleeve (and no, they don't involve catnip, though I hear that stuff is pretty mind-expanding).

1. Surround yourself with diverse perspectives

One of the biggest threats to curiosity is homogeneity: surrounding yourself with people who think like you, talk like you, and see the world the same way you do. It's comfortable, sure, but it's also a surefire way to get stuck in your own echo chamber.

So make a point of seeking out diverse perspectives and experiences. Hire people who challenge your assumptions and bring fresh ideas to the table. Collaborate with teams and individuals from different backgrounds, industries, and disciplines. Attend conferences and events that push you out of your comfort zone and expose you to new ways of thinking.

The more diverse your network and your inputs, the more likely you are to encounter new questions and ideas that keep your curiosity alive and well.

2. Embrace the beginner's mind

When you're an expert in your field, it's easy to fall into the trap of thinking you know it all.

But expertise can be a double-edged sword; while it gives you a deep understanding of your subject matter, it can also create blind spots and biases that limit your curiosity.

That's where a beginner's mind comes in. The beginner's mind is a concept from Zen Buddhism that refers to approaching every situation with openness, eagerness, and a lack of preconceptions, just like a beginner would.

So how do you cultivate a beginner's mind, even when you're a seasoned pro? Start by questioning your own assumptions and biases. Ask yourself, "What if I'm wrong about this? What if there's another way of looking at it?" Approach every situation with a sense of wonder and humility, as if you're seeing it for the first time.

In addition, do not hesitate to pose "dumb" inquiries—namely, those that may induce feelings of inexperience. Those are often the questions that lead to the biggest breakthroughs and the most surprising insights.

3. Make time for play and experimentation

Curiosity thrives on play and experimentation—the freedom to tinker, to try new things, to follow your whims and see where they lead. But as we get older and more "serious" in our roles, it's easy to lose touch with that sense of playfulness and creativity.

So make a point of building play and experimentation into your routine. Set aside time each week (or even each day) for unstructured exploration and idea generation. Encourage your team to do the same, and create a culture where it's okay to try new things and fail forward.

And don't be afraid to get a little weird with it. Have a "crazy idea" brainstorming session where no idea is too wild or too wacky. Play improv games to get your creative juices flowing. Take a field trip to a museum, a park, or a local business and look for inspiration in unexpected places.

The more you embrace play and experimentation,

the more you'll keep your curiosity muscles flexible and ready for action.

4. Stay uncomfortable

Comfort is the enemy of curiosity. When we're comfortable, we're not motivated to seek out new experiences or challenge ourselves to grow. We're like cats curled up in a sunny spot, content to snooze the day away.

So if you want to stay curious, you've got to stay uncomfortable. That means pushing yourself out of your comfort zone on a regular basis. Taking on new challenges and responsibilities. Learning new skills and exploring new domains. Traveling to new places and immersing yourself in new cultures.

It also means getting comfortable with discomfort—the discomfort of not knowing, of being wrong, of failing and trying again. Embrace the awkward, the uncertain, and the unfamiliar. Lean into the discomfort and see where it takes you.

Because here's the thing: discomfort is where growth happens. It's where curiosity thrives. It's where the magic happens (and no, I'm not talking about the kind of magic that involves pulling rabbits out of hats, though that would be pretty darn impressive).

5. Ask "What if?" and "Why not?"

Finally, if you want to stay curious, you've got to keep asking the big questions—the ones that challenge the status quo and imagine new possibilities. And two of the most powerful questions in your curiosity toolkit are "What if?" and "Why not?"

"What if?" is the question that opens up new worlds

and new ways of thinking. It's the question that takes you from "this is how it's always been done" to "this is how it could be done." It's the question that sparks your imagination and sets your curiosity on fire.

"Why not?" is the question that challenges assumptions and pushes boundaries. It's the question that takes you from "that'll never work" to "let's give it a shot." It's the question that emboldens you to take risks and try new things, even when the odds seem stacked against you.

So make a habit of asking "what if?" and "why not?" on a regular basis. Ask them about your products, your processes, your industry, and your world. Ask them about the biggest challenges you're facing and the wildest dreams you've never dared to pursue.

And then listen to the answers. Follow the trail of curiosity wherever it leads you. Because that's how you stay curious, even when you're the cat's meow. That's how you keep growing, keep innovating, and keep discovering new possibilities and new horizons.

And who knows? Maybe one day you'll find yourself in a sunny spot, curled up like a contented cat, purring with satisfaction at all the amazing things you've learned and accomplished. But even then, don't forget to keep one eye open for the next big question, the next great adventure.

Because curiosity, my friend, is the key to staying forever young, forever hungry, and forever in love with the world and all its wonders.

So go forth and stay curious. Keep questioning. Keep

exploring. Keep chasing after the "what if?"s and the "why not?"s. And never, ever stop being the cat's meow.

Remember, a cat has whiskers in part, so it never gets into a tight squeeze it can't get back out of. And with that, I'll leave you with one final question: What will you ask today?

Do stuff. Be clenched, curious.
Not waiting for inspiration's shove
or society's kiss on your forehead.
- Susan Sontag

Curiousity Didn't Kill the Cat, it Made Her CEO

8

Cultivating Your Team's Potential, Not Just Their Performance

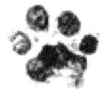

"Why are cats smarter than dogs?
It's simple: Humans train dogs.
Whereas cats see he potential in their humans and train them.
I make sure my human knows that I need a nice indoor litter tray in the sun, fancy cat food, and play time at two in the morning.
Nurture your colleagues' curiosity; you want them to playfully explore and gain new insights. I am not waiting for you to click your fingers and give them a treat for doing the right thing. That's quite literally a dog's life."

Tigris, Aurora (2020), The Five-Hour Nap Rule

We've explored the ins and outs of wielding questions like a pro. But there's another piece of the leadership puzzle that deserves a laser pointer: the art of nurturing your team's potential, not just their performance.

But wait, aren't KPIs the holy grail of leadership?

By now, hopefully we all know that when we focus solely on performance, we're essentially creating a negative consequence if the team does not meet expectations. Sure, they might jump a little higher next time to avoid disappointment, but they're not exactly inspired to bring their A-game. When you put all your eggs in the "accountability" basket, you often end up with a team of unmotivated, or even disgruntled, cats who are just not likely to go the extra mile to meet the company's larger goals.

When you focus on what they're doing right and their potential, you nurture your team's inherent awesomeness, and you'll watch them blossom. Treat your people like the rock stars they actually are, and they'll take ownership of their work faster than a cat claiming a new cardboard box.

True story: When my first boss started fostering my potential and growth, instead of focusing on my lack of experience, I went from zero to hero faster than you can say "catnip." It was in a design studio, and suddenly, I was questioning everything, taking risks, and creating wine label designs that not only broke the mold but were getting accepted by our clients. It left the others in the studio wondering if I'd been sipping the good stuff.

The moral of this little story? Support everything

your team does well. They will be able to leap over tall obstacles in a single bound, solve problems at the speed of a speeding bullet, and generally be the savage cats you always suspected they could be. They will be able to leap over tall obstacles in a single bound, solve problems at the speed of a speeding bullet, and generally be the savage cats you always suspected they could be.

Now, I'm not saying performance doesn't matter. Of course, you need to make sure everyone's pulling their weight, so it is a fine balancing act. But when you make strengths and potential the main attractions and shortcomings the sideshow, that's when the real magic happens.

So, how can you become the ringleader of this strength-celebrating circus? Here are a few tricks that'll make you the cat's meow:

1. Ask questions that make your team feel like superheroes. Instead of "Are you sure you can handle this?" try "What's your secret sauce for nailing this project?"

2. Let your team roam free and explore their wild ideas. You never know when a crazy notion might turn into a game-changing innovation.

3. Celebrate when your team members try something really innovative or progressive, even if they fail. Promote learning from failures as a path to fulfilling potential.

4. Use questions to uncover your team's hidden talents. Ask them, "What skills do you have that we haven't tapped into yet?" or "What projects would you love to sink your claws into?"

5. When faced with a challenge, ask your team, "How can we use our collective strengths to claw our way to victory?" This shifts the focus from individual shortcomings to team power.
6. During one-on-one check-ins, ask your team members, "What accomplishments are you most proud of this week?" and "What strengths did you flex to make that happen?" Celebrate their wins and help them see their own greatness.
7. Finally, always be the curious cat you want to see in the world. When you're constantly learning, growing, and pushing your own boundaries, your team will follow suit.

The most famous proponent of this style of leadership is Google. Since its inception, Google's co-founders, Larry Page and Sergey Brin, have recognized the importance of nurturing innovation as a key driver of their company's success. When people work on things they are passionate about, they tend to be more motivated and productive.

In the wise words of a certain fabulous feline, "Leadership isn't about being the boss; it's about being the catalyst for your team's brilliance."

If anyone gives you flack for being too "soft" on your team, just remember: you're not herding cats; you're unleashing tigers.

Though if you're unleashing tigers, ask yourself how you're getting them back in the cage. And not getting eaten, especially if you want to be a zookeeper. It's the question they ask at the job interview, and if you don't have an answer. You'll only get the answer if they want to save money on tiger food and you are lunch.

Creativity is not just for artists.
It's for business people looking
for a new way to close a sale.
It's for engineers trying
to solve a problem.
It's for parents who want their
children to see the world
in more than one way.
— Twyla Tharp

Curiousity Didn't Kill the Cat, it Made Her CEO

Final Thoughts

Questioning Your Way to the Top

There's a reason people say that someone who is satisfied looks like "the cat that got the cream.". And that's not just because cream is nice. It's because it took effort, cunning curiosity, planning, and an occasional bitten ankle to reach their goal. You just need to get into the habit of asking the right questions, being open to the right answer, and the fine art of puking the occasional hairball into a pair of Louboutins (or is that more of a cat thing?).

Just remember its curiosity that skilled the cat.

Curiousity Didn't Kill the Cat, it Made Her CEO

Well, my inquisitive friend, we've come to the end of our journey through the wacky, wonderful world of curiosity. We've explored the power of questions, the art of active listening, the thrill of embracing the unknown, and the joy of staying forever young and hungry for knowledge.

But before we bid each other adieu and ride off into the sunset of intellectual fulfillment (like a cat on a rainbow unicorn, naturally), let's take a moment to reflect on what we've learned and what lies ahead.

Because here's the thing: curiosity isn't just a nice-to-have; it's a fun little extra that makes life a bit more interesting. It's a superpower, a secret weapon, and a magic elixir that can transform your lives, your work, and your world in ways you never imagined possible.

Think about it: all the greatest innovators, the most groundbreaking inventors, and the most visionary leaders throughout history have one thing in common: an insatiable curiosity, a relentless desire to ask questions, to challenge assumptions, and to explore new frontiers.

From Leonardo da Vinci to Albert Einstein, from Marie Curie to Steve Jobs, the world's most brilliant minds have always been the ones who never stopped asking "why?" and "what if?" and "how can we make this better?" They're the ones who looked at the world around them and saw not just what was, but what could be—and then set out to make it happen.

And that, my dear reader, is the power of curiosity. It's the power to see beyond the status quo, to imagine new possibilities, and to create something extraordinary out of the ordinary. It's the power to lead with questions, to inspire others to join you on a quest for knowledge and discovery, to change the game, and to rewrite the rules.

But here's the thing: curiosity isn't just for geniuses and visionaries. It's for everyone. It's for you, right here, right now, in whatever role, industry, or life stage you find yourself in. Because no matter who you are or what you do, curiosity is the key to unlocking your full potential and achieving your wildest dreams.

So, how do you do it? How do you question your way to the top—to the life, career, and impact you've always wanted?

It starts with a mindset shift—a fundamental reframing of how you approach the world and your place in it. Instead of seeing yourself as a passive recipient of knowledge and expertise, start seeing yourself as an active seeker, a curious explorer, and a lifelong learner who's always hungry for more.

Embrace the beginner's mind—the sense of wonder, openness, and eagerness that comes from approaching every situation as if it's the first time. Ask "dumb" questions—the ones that might make you feel like a total newbie but can lead to the most surprising insights and breakthroughs.

Surround yourself with diverse perspectives and experiences, with people and ideas that challenge your assumptions and push you out of your comfort zone. Seek out the unfamiliar, the uncomfortable, and the unknown, because that's where magic happens, where curiosity thrives and innovation is born.

Make time for play and experimentation, for unstructured exploration, and for idea generation. Give yourself permission to tinker, to try new things, to follow your whims and see where they lead. And don't be afraid to fail, because failure is just another opportunity to learn, to grow, to ask new questions, and to find new answers.

And above all, keep asking, "What if?" and "Why not?" Keep pushing the boundaries of what's possible; keep imagining new worlds and new ways of being. Keep chasing after the biggest, boldest, most audacious questions you can think of, because that's how you change the game, how you make your mark, and how you leave a legacy that lasts.

So go forth and question, my brilliant friend. Question everything, always, with an open mind and an open heart. Question your way to the top, to the life, career, and impact you've always dreamed of.

And remember, curiosity may have killed the cat, but it's the very thing that will keep you alive—alive to the wonders, possibilities, and adventures that await you at every turn.

So here's to staying curious, to leading with questions, to embracing the unknown and chasing after the "what if?"s and the "why not?"s. Here's to being the kind of leader, the kind of innovator, the kind of human being who never stops learning, never stops growing, never stops asking the big questions, and never stops dreaming the big dreams.

Because in the end, that's what it's all about—not just questioning your way to the top, but questioning your way to a life well-lived, a life full of wonder and discovery and joy and meaning. A life that matters, that makes a difference, and that leaves the world a little bit better than you found it.

And if you can do that, my curious compadre, then you'll be the cat's meow indeed (I know, I know, I said I was done with the cat puns, but I just couldn't resist one last hurrah).

So here's to you: to your curiosity, to your quest for knowledge, and to your thirst for adventure. May your questions be bold, your insights be brilliant, and your impact be boundless.

And may you always, always keep asking, "Why?" and "What if?" and "How can we make this better?" because that, in the end, is the true secret to success, happiness, and a life well lived.

So go forth and ask, my friend. The world is waiting for you.

…mic drop.

(Just kidding, I would never drop a microphone; those things are expensive, and I'm a curious but frugal cat!)

P.S. I hope you enjoyed reading this as much as we did writting it, would love your thoughts in a review!

Curiousity Didn't Kill the Cat, it Made Her CEO

Appendix

Top Cat Tips

This book is meant to be short and sweet, but packed full of juicy goodness. To make it even easier to build questions into your daily life and leadership duties, Aurora has made the following little cheat sheet for your reference.

Exploratory Questions:
- "What's the biggest obstacle you're facing in your work right now?"
- "If you could change one thing about our team's process, what would it be?"
- "What do you think our competitors are doing better than us?"

Guiding Questions:
- "What if we tried [your idea] as a solution to this problem?"
- "How might [your idea] help us achieve our goals faster?"
- "What would be the benefits of implementing [your idea]?"

Evaluative Questions:
- "How does this project align with our quarterly goals?"
- "What metrics are you using to measure success?"
- "What steps have you taken to mitigate the risks we discussed?"

Questions To Get Your Team To Open Up:
- "What's been the most challenging part of this project for you?"
- "How do you feel about the changes we've been making to our process?"
- "What do you think is holding our team back from reaching our full potential?"
- "Can you give me an example of a time when you felt frustrated with our team's communication?"
- "What do you think is the root cause of the delays we've been experiencing?"
- "How do you think we could improve our team's collaboration and coordination?"

Questions To Uncover Productivity Issues:
- "On a scale of 1-10, how would you rate your motivation and engagement lately?"
- "What do you think is the biggest obstacle to our team's productivity right now?"
- "If you could wave a magic wand and change one thing about our team's workflow, what would it be?"
- "What tasks or projects have been taking longer

than expected lately?"
- "Are there any tools or resources you feel like you're missing that could help you be more productive?"
- "How could we streamline our communication and decision-making processes to be more efficient?"

Open-Ended Questions:
- "What challenges are you currently facing in your role?"
- "How might we improve our team's communication skills?"
- "What projects are you most excited about?"
- "How can we make our team meetings more engaging than a laser pointer show?"

Closed-Ended Questions:
- "Did you meet that deadline as planned?"
- "How many sales calls did you make last week?"

Crafting Questions That Make Your Team's Brains Hurt (in a Good Way):
- "What would happen if we approached this problem from the opposite direction?"
- "How might we redesign this process from scratch to make it 10 times more efficient?"
- "What assumptions are we making about our customers that might be holding us back?"

Using Questions to Guide Your Team Through Problem-Solving:
- "What specifically is not working with our

current approach?"
- "What data or evidence do we have that supports this?"
- "Why do we think this problem is occurring in the first place?"
- "What are some potential solutions we haven't considered yet?"
- "How might we test or validate these ideas before implementing them?"
- "What resources or support would we need to make this solution a reality?"
- "What do you think is the biggest challenge you're facing with this project right now?"
- "What steps could you take to overcome that challenge and get the project back on track?"
- "What did we do well on this project, and what could we have done better?"

Promoting Constructive Dialogue and Debate:
- "What might someone with a completely different background or expertise say about this issue?"
- "How might our competitors or customers view this situation differently than we do?"
- "What are some potential unintended consequences or risks of this approach that we haven't considered?"

Performance-Gauging Questions:
- "What do you think are your biggest strengths and areas for improvement when it comes to

[specific skill or task]?"
- "How would you rate your performance on [a project or initiative] on a scale of 1–10, and why?"
- "What feedback have you received from colleagues or stakeholders about your work on [the project or initiative]?"

Coaching Questions:
- "What do you think is holding you back from reaching your goals in this area?"
- "What steps could you take to overcome that obstacle and make progress?"
- "How can I support you in implementing that plan and holding yourself accountable?"

Empowering Your Team to Ask Evaluative Questions:
- "What did I do well on this project, and what could I have done better?"
- "How did my work on this initiative contribute to the overall goals of the team or organization?"
- "What feedback or suggestions do you have for me based on your experience working with me on this project?"

Best Practices for Formulating Questions:
- "What roadblocks are you currently facing in meeting the project deadline?"
- "If we go down this path, what monsters might we unleash?"
- "What specific line items are you most worried

about, and why?"

Questioning for When You're in a Crisis:

- "What do we know for sure about what happened?"
- "What are the most immediate risks we need to mitigate?"
- "What are some potential solutions we could implement right now?"

Questioning for When You're Dealing With Conflict:

- "What do you think is the root cause of this disagreement?"
- "How do you think the other person is feeling about this situation?"
- "What would a win-win solution look like for both of you?"

Questioning for When You Have No Idea What You're Doing:

- "I have to admit, I'm not an expert in this area. Can you help me understand the key issues at play?"
- "What are some best practices or examples from other organizations that we could learn from?"
- "Who else in the company might have valuable insights or expertise to share on this topic?"

Ask Yourself Self-Reflective Questions:

- "What assumptions am I making about myself, my team, or my business?"
- "What would I do differently if I was more

curious and less certain?"
- "What questions am I afraid to ask, and why?"
- "How can I push myself out of my comfort zone and keep growing as a leader?"

*It is always with excitement
that I wake up in the morning
wondering what my intuition will
toss up to me, like gifts from the
sea. Intuition tells the thinking
mind where to look next.
– Jonas Salk*

How To Make Friends and Be Purrsuasive

Ask Questions that Reveal Your Own Knowledge Gaps:
- Invite dissenting opinions and thank people for challenging your ideas.
- Share your own "aha" moments of discovery and growth.

Encouraging Your Team to Question Everything:
- Make "Do you have any questions?" your new favorite catchphrase.
- Publicly reward people who speak up with tough or thought-provoking questions.
- Ban the phrase "this is how we've always done it."

Strategies for Developing Questioning Skills:
- Host regular "question storming" sessions where people brainstorm provocative questions about a project or problem.

- Create a "Questions Hall of Fame" to showcase examples of killer questions that led to breakthroughs.
- Offer professional development workshops on techniques like Socratic questioning, appreciative inquiry, and humble inquiry.

Questioning Accelerates Learning, Adaptability, and Performance By:

- Building new neural pathways, challenging assumptions, and expanding mental models
- Empowering teams to think for themselves, take risks, and try new things
- Unleashing potential, facilitating idea flow, and problem-solving

Embracing Questioning as a Core Leadership Competency:

- Lightens the load of leadership while maintaining authenticity
- Models vulnerability and openness
- Engages the team in co-creation and collaboration
- Welcomes diverse perspectives and new ways of thinking

About the Author

Sheli Bowman, a conscious business strategist and entrepreneur, left corporate life to guide other purpose-driven entrepreneurs, coaches, and wellness experts to share their wisdom and make an impact.

Since co-founding a web development company in 1996 (when the internet was still mainly for Star Trek forums), Sheli has been the creative director, brand manager, or digital strategy consultant for multinationals. She's also had her own digital agency, a health food store (kale chips, anyone?), and was CEO of a wellness Web3 project.

Armed with an MBA and a unique blend of strategic and spiritual wisdom, when not writing leadership strategy books, Sheli runs course creation and business strategy coaching programs (more at sheli.com). She's also a Reiki Master (27yrs), reads the Akashic Records, and facilitates other modalities.

Daily meditation and walks in nature keep her mostly sane, though her philosophical debates with trees are a bit worrying. When not indulging her lifelong love of travel, Sheli calls home a little island in the South China Sea, along with her husband Humphrey and little cat Otti - who, despite her best efforts, still prefers tuna to TED talks.

.

The travel impulse is mental and physical curiosity. It's a passion. And I can't understand people who don't want to travel.
– Paul Thoreaux

Coming Soon!

Please look out for these upcoming leadership stratergy books, also by Sheli Bowman (sorry, no cat allegories):

Mastering AI Leadership: May the Bots Be with You

A Strategic Guide of Well-Caffeinated Jedi Wisdom

The line separating science fiction from reality is thinner in this age of Artificial Intelligence than it would be following a unicorn sighting. Not only are our phones and self-driving cars smart, but our modest office equipment is starting to participate. Indeed, your coffee maker may be the most intelligent member of your staff (it most likely boasts a stronger work ethic as well).

This strategic guide equips leaders with the knowledge and strategies needed to thrive in the age of artificial intelligence. The author emphasizes the profound impact of AI on the workplace, projecting trillions in economic growth, and underscores the evolving role of leadership and ethics in this rapidly transforming landscape. The book provides a roadmap for successfully integrating AI into an organization, from building an AI-savvy toolkit to fostering a culture of innovation and adaptability.

Leaders learn practical steps like cultivating curiosity about AI advancements, starting with small pilots, and prioritizing ethical considerations around bias, privacy, and transparency. Real-world case studies illustrate how companies are leveraging AI to drive efficiency, enhance decision-making, and create competitive advantages.

Crucially, the author highlights the enduring value of uniquely human skills like emotional intelligence, creativity, and ethical judgment in an increasingly automated world. Strategies for maintaining authentic connections, celebrating human contributions, and balancing AI's efficiency with the need for purpose and meaning empower leaders to guide their organizations into the future, where humans and AI collaborate to achieve unprecedented innovation and success.

Perfectly Scattered:
The ADHD Executive's Guide to Thrive

From Chaos to Clarity,
Strategies for Neurodivergent Success

This strategic guide for ADHD leaders offers an insightful and irreverent journey through harnessing the superpowers of the neurodiverse brain. The author, an ADHD coach who's intimately acquainted with the "Ooh, shiny!" brain, reframes ADHD not as a disorder, but as a unique neurological

Coming Soon!

wiring that comes with its own set of competitive advantages in the modern business world. Far from being a total liability, the ADHD brain's tendency towards rapid ideation, adaptability, and thirst for novelty are positioned as the keys to innovation and disruptive leadership.

The book dives into practical strategies for leveraging ADHD traits across various aspects of executive management. Readers learn techniques for channeling hyperfocus, optimizing creativity, and transforming emotional intensity into a leadership superpower.

Peppered throughout are real-world case studies and the author's signature brand of tongue-in-cheek humor, making this guide as entertaining as it is enlightening. Recognizing that the ADHD brain doesn't always play nicely with traditional management advice, the book champions a refreshingly neurodiversity-friendly approach.

ADHD leaders are empowered to turn their "squirrel moments" into eureka-worthy breakthroughs, their impulsivity into strategic advantages, and their emotional intensity into an unparalleled capacity for empathetic, authentic leadership. So, grab your favorite fidget toy, embrace your perfectly scattered mind, and get ready to lead your organization to new heights - with plenty of creativity, laughter, and strategically timed caffeine breaks along the way. ADHD: Absolutely Delivering High Disruption (or, as the French say...TADAHHHHH!)..

.

Pandemic Pivot: How COVID Changed Leadership Forever (and What to Do About It)

A Survivor's Guide to Chaos, Confusion, and Copious Amounts of Hand Sanitizer

This is an insightful guide to navigating the tumultuous waters of leadership during and after the COVID-19 pandemic. Author Sheli Bowman combines humor with practical advice to explore how the global crisis has fundamentally altered the landscape of leadership. This book takes readers on a journey through the chaos of the early pandemic days, the challenges of remote work, and the lasting impact on organizational culture and management practices. With chapters covering topics like virtual communication, empathetic leadership, and preparing for future crises, Bowman offers a comprehensive look at the "new normal" of leadership. Written in an engaging and relatable style, "Pandemic Pivot" provides valuable lessons and strategies for leaders at all levels who are grappling with the ongoing effects of the pandemic on their teams and organizations. It's a must-read for anyone looking to thrive in the post-pandemic world of work, offering both laughs and practical insights along the way.